The Other Side of The Counter

By:

Michael P. Ward

Introduction:

I decided to write this book after four years of college learning about poor customer service, and one year living it. Whenever we hear about a person experiencing horrible customer service we remember it and use it to make decisions. How many times have you wanted to get something to eat and find yourself stopping from going to a particular restaurant because someone you know spoke poorly of the place? Now how many times have you asked yourself why the person you knew received the customer service they did?

We never do, no matter how much of an ass, our friend, coworkers, or relatives are we never ask, " *I wonder what Ben did to receive such poor service"*. When two kids get into a fight, or a man or a women have a child we know both people are the cause of the end result. If you are reading this book and currently or in the past worked in retail and have had an escalation with a customer where a manager has stepped in how many times did he or she just assume that you were at fault. Likewise, when you had a disagreement with a co-worker management sits both of you down hears both sides of the story than makes a decision about who is right or wrong. I am not going to write this book to beat up on the company or management, it is apparent I am obliviously not a corporate Kool-aid drinker but *"yes men"* are the main cause of the problem. Always remember in life average people don't rock the boat because they want to jump aboard it. Rather than do the right thing not only providing great customer service we do whatever we can to make customers happy rather than set the correct expectations. Furthermore, this book titled *The Other Side of The Counter* tells the story from a retail workers point of view as to why a customer received horrible service, or why certain products are forced on to you the customers.

Chapter: 1 Own up to the situation

A typical Sunday morning, rolling our eyes in frustration at the site of zombies lingering at the front door. Being experienced retail employees we know on a typical Sunday morning that customers rather than getting up early to purchase a device rather get to the store as early as possible to return one or because their device isn't working. It's the last thing we want to do this early in the morning, one because the majority of us were out on the town to all hours of the night on Saturday, two we work off commission but usually service devices around 80% of the time rather than sell them (just a wild guess actually on the 80%). Finally, customers purchase a device from one sales rep but almost always get it serviced by another one, which prompts retail employees to ask themselves why do customers never come back and ask for the same sales rep.

About the most frustrating task anyone has to do in a retail location is service or troubleshoot a device you spoke to a customer for over two hours about just to watch them purchase it from another sales rep on a different day. What is even more frustrating is when the customer has a problem with their phone and now suddenly remembers how amazing you were and decides to come speak to you about the devices problem. Any sales rep who has ever experienced this can honestly tell you they would rather tell the customer to go fly a kite. In reality though whose fault is it really, and where is the disconnect when it comes to selling and retail.

One day I was having a conversation with one of my coworkers who was not known for being a high sales performer but rather a very low performer. Needless to say I hardly ever took anything he had to say seriously or pay attention to either (when talking about sales, I like the guy a lot personally). Needing someone to vent to I stood next to him standing at the front of the store waiting for the next customer to walk into the store. I had just watched a customer I spent an hour with two days earlier add two lines of service with another sales rep who did nothing at all to sell the product but was sure going to get commission for being an order taker. Makes me wonder why we don't just slash cost and hire a bunch of checkout clerks from the local grocery store; at the current moment it seemed to make a lot of sense. Without thinking I had to vent out of mere frustration "I CANT BELIEVE I JUST

SPENT AN HOUR WITH THOSE PEOPLE AND THEY CAME IN AND DIDN'T ASK FOR ME, WHY IS IT THAT CUSTOMERS NEVER COME BACK IN AND ASK FOR THE PERSON THAT HELPED THEM THEY JUST TAKE ANYBODY, BUT IM SURE AS SOON AS THAT DEVICE NEEDS SERVICING THEY WILL COME FIND ME." Sean being the calm collected intelligent thinker he is just sighed looked at me and said " Michael I agree with you a 100% its nerve racking, but how often do we take other peoples sales or end up servicing another reps devices. Its our fault because we don't hold reps accountable for there actions, we end up always servicing their customers equipment and never bring it to there attention. Instead we just get pissed off become passive aggressive and end up hating life".

It is almost like a game of dominos if you really think about it, by dominos I mean the rippling effect it can have on everyone. Case in point, I was setting up my station ready to set a family up on a new family plan. All of a sudden a very large man comes up to me approaches me with a brown box in his hand. Working in retail I know it could only be one thing, his phone needs activating because he wasn't smart enough to read the activation instructions that come in the box printed in **36 point**

font! Imagine day after day having to activate

peoples replacement devices, it becomes as much as
second nature as shooting a rifle is to a private in the
marine corps. So when the first thing that came out of
this customer's mouth was " I tried to activate it at
home but it was to difficult and I couldn't
figure out how"(you would be surprised how
difficult it is to put a sim card in a device). If
it wasn't for the fact I have to provide
customer service I would have rolled my eyes and called him
an idiot. Instead I politely asked him if he had been
checked in to the que, but before I could explain further
he became irate. To avoid and escalation I decided just to
help the customer assuming it wouldn't take more than five
minutes, however I was about to find out I wasn't going
anywhere for awhile.

When I asked to see the box with his replacement phone
in it he gave me two phones, two different phones which is
always an indication of a customer who escalated a problem
to a manager for well lets just say a really good reason
(sarcasm). I was planning on skipping the whole question

of why he had two different phones for the sake of time, but the customer decided how important it was to tell me a detailed ten-minute history of his problem. He immediately pointed to the direction of a sales rep who may or may not be known for dumping tech off on other reps explaining how when he walked in he had every intention of being helped by the same rep who service him before but when they made eye contact she b- lined it to the back of the store where the offices where at. He explained he was given a temporary phone because he was a truck driver and needed it to keep in contact with his company and use for a GPS. He was just really confused since the last rep had told him he could just transfer memory cards and it would activate just fine. I was beginning to understand why he was so frustrated and began to feel bad about getting aggravated that I had to service someone else's device.

He now had two phones, two sd cards which are used to store information, and two sim cards that are used to power smartphones with wireless service. I can completely understand why he was now confused, who wouldn't be if they didn't work in my profession everyday. Confused about the difference between the sd card and the sim card he was afraid he would make a mistake and break the replacement phone. Not to mention the sim cards where two different sizes and he didn't know which one to use, I guess the fact there was not a space for the small one was no indication that it probably just didn't belong in the replacement phone. However, beside the obvious fact that not all the cards would fit into the replacement device we as sales rep speak in what I like to call *jargon* to customers assuming that they should understand what we do.

I see it all the time when dealing with customers who need their devices serviced. Reps speak in jargon trying desperately to get rid of the customer so they can move on to the next person in line in the hopes it is a sale. We use terms like CLNR, D-FILL, and sim card, simple terms we say 10,000 times a day we just assume customers understand as easily as we do. What one rep uses to get rid of a customer to suit their needs in reality ends up causing a rippling effect for others in this case the current customer, my appointment, as well as myself.

Midway through helping this customer I looked out the corner of my eye and saw my customer staring at me trying to get my attention to let me know they were here and waiting for me. I was supposed already be helping her so I politely told her I would be there in a few minutes. What

I didn't know was that this customer lost all of his music on his device and the last sales rep told him that we could put his music back on his phone. Like everything else you simply cant tell a customer sorry I'm not trained to do this and refer them elsewhere and expect them to just except it. Really cant blame them either to be completely honest either after all someone has to help them, you don't exactly learn multiplication on your own. However, that is exactly what came out of my mouth and as a result opened the floodgates to a world of why not questions from the customer. If I had just explained to him why I could not help him and show him were he could have gone to get help it might have been an easier process. Well I didn't and as a result had to suffer the wrath of an angry customer. Anxiously trying to move on to my appointment I kept glancing over to see if my customer was still there, each look I could see less and less patience in her in her body language. Instead of going over to a manager and requesting someone else to help my customer I made the mistake of just trying to hurry through one customer to get to my appointment. Furthermore, my appointment left without setting up service, the company lost an added customer and the current customer I was helping left the store not accomplishing what he had actually intended.

I was furious, asking myself why did the last sales rep just tell this customer someone could put his music back on his phone knowing we don't provide these services in the store. Better yet why could the sales rep that sold him this phone just service the damn thing? Because of their laziness it cost me a sale and I got yelled at for an hour straight. I wanted to walk directly over to the sales rep who caused this fiasco and ask her "why did you tell the customer this" "why didn't you set up an appointment to help him" "when you saw him why didn't you come take over". Instead I decided to go to lunch to cool off and try to forget it ever happened and move on. Well that didn't happen, but what did happen is I started thinking about what I could have done to make the situation better. Rather than getting frustrated and letting it affect my work, I could have gotten a manager to assist the other customer and ensured the current customer had a good experience and done as much as I could to see that I helped him with his problem. As I stated earlier people just don't accept what you tell them and move on, the same principal applies when someone wrongs you and you have to deal with it and they get off scotch free. It eats away at you and want to somehow get back at them to even the odds. Except you cant, all you can ever do is accept what has happened and move on, it didn't hurt the other sales rep one bit that it cost me a sale and a world of frustration; you just have to accept the fact that what goes around comes around. Furthermore, I still think the whole fiasco could have been avoided had the rep set the right expectation from the start and since she failed to do this it caused a domino effect that caused other customers a negative experience.

The next day I came into the store not upset, but I did ask to speak to my manager in her office to discuss how to avoid this problem from happening again. It wasn't out of the ordinary for other reps to complain about this particular sales rep so I wanted to make a point not to make it about her but rather the situation. My manager is a delightful lady who always tries to bring out the best in us, its one of the many things I love and respect about her. One month our store ended in the red and was their for the majority of the month and she was still as delightful as could be trying to motivate us rather than taking her frustration out on us for not performing well. Although her and I argue almost every single day mostly because we are two type A personalities we always seem to keep respecting and understanding one another. Because she knows me so well she knows I like to speak more often than I like to listen or that fact I'm just a narcissist (not a great quality to have in a person but hey were all human after all).

I began to explain not about the particular instance that had happened the day before but the growing disconnect between customers and retail sales employees. In any other profession customers always contact their sales rep, if you are buying a home you contact the realtor helping you, if you are selling pharmaceuticals to a doctor they will contact the sales rep who sold them the product; if they have a problem (that could be for other reasons pertaining to how attractive she is but hey that's why companies higher them). However, customers never seem to consistently come back and ask for the same sales rep when it comes to cellphones. It's not the fact we provide terrible customer service, don't give customers our business cards, or set the expectations that by continuing to work with the same rep is more convenient and easy for customers **when coming back for a sale**. I went on to explain how I overheard a customer once ask a sales rep why we never want to help customers out when we come in to see what phone we like but want to purchase on a different day.

I explained how much I wanted to walk over to that particular customer and tell them it was because we spend hours going over devices with them just to watch them purchase it from another rep. Afterwards, I gave an example of me speaking to a lady who had a family of five looking to add service with our company. I spent a little over two hours with her going over price plans, devices, global options, gave her my business card and informed her to set up an appointment when she was ready to purchase. A week later I walked into work and came to find she had purchased the devices from another sales rep. Furthermore, my manager wasn't nearly as sympathetic as I thought she was going to be.

As any man knows when a women crosses her arms and isn't smiling it generally isn't considered an invite to dinner. It also means you need to shut your mouth and listen to what she has to say. In my case it meant I should have just got up out of the chair and gone back to work. However, I was stubborn enough to listen to what she had to say, although I came to learn a very valuable lesson.

In a very stern tone of voice she addressed fact that sales rep will always go out of there way for a customer when selling them a device, but when it comes to servicing equipment were always willing to pass it off or simply ignore them. In all honesty she is correct, we both agreed it is what annoys us both when we overhear reps push service out the door simply because they are too lazy to actually fix the device. What we didn't agree on is how to go about changing the culture amongst all of the sales reps in the store. My idea was to start setting expectations with customers to always come back in and ask for the same sales rep. If they were to walk in their options would be to get an appointment set up to be assisted by that rep, or for us to send that sales rep an email informing them of the situation and have them contact the customer. Likewise, my manager disagreed completely stating we need to own every situation in store and cant have customers waiting for days for a rep to contact them nor could management micro manage every situation to see if reps were actually following up with their customers (we already don't for the most part to be completely honest).

As much as I would like to think my recommendation is correct about setting expectations my managers were more correct in this instance. Not that she used these exact terms but what she was explaining to me where the differences between discrete exchanges and relationship exchanges. The problem was as sales reps selling devices and not servicing them but having someone else do it so we weren't developing a relationship with our customers. This culture had existed well since the existence of the company dating back twelve years. We created a culture of selling devices and making customers jump through hoops for getting their devices serviced. Now the transition from discrete exchange to relationship exchanges from an academic standpoint is to do a few quick fix steps and make a habit of it. However, convincing sales reps to start servicing devices they sell to customer is the equivalent to convincing France to switch their economic policies from socialism to capitalism (i.e. its not gonna happen). All I can do is move forward from this point creating relationships with my customers hoping to inspire my fellow co-workers with the success I receive as a result; for now I will have to write another chapter of this book to tell you how it works out.

Chapter 2: A salesman is not a businessman

When I was in college I often wondered why more sales classes were not taught in the curriculum. After all salesmen are the ones on the front lines bringing in revenue for the company and most college graduates aren't going to start their careers out developing strategies for front line workers to execute in the field. Like my good friend Tom Gallegoes an army veteran of three tours in Iraq once told me "mike you've got to be a private before you can become an NCO. However, I have come to find that salespeople are not business people, which is why more classes are not taught in business colleges.

This is not a problem that has to be researched by scholars and researchers alike. The answer is pretty simple actually; commissions and a balance scorecard corrupt salespeople. Now I am not completely against commissions or scorecards as they do in theory serve a good purpose (as does universal healthcare but hey lets not get into politics). Its just when it comes doing what is right for customers rather than a paycheck or the company salesperson for the most part do what is better for their paychecks rather than what customers actually want. Ron

Johnson, Senior Vice President of Retail at Apple said it best, " I don't want a sales person looking at your wallet. I want them looking at your heart."

Having a scorecard to sell by and commissions to work on prohibits sales rep in my company from doing just that. I completely see and understand why businesses have a balance scorecard and why they pay reps more in commissions for selling products that align with the scorecard. Businesses are for profit companies looking to maximize the shareholder wealth and the bottom line, which they should do. However selling a product you get scored and payed more on that nobody wants is the same as trying to convince a liberal capitalism is better for society than socialism.

I see it every single day when at work a customer walks in wanting this particular device or product that the rep doesn't get paid or can get paid more on another they bring the pressure. Opening up with statements like *well why do you want that*" or "*have you heard about this new product*" which they should since after all they are sales reps and it is their job to discover needs rather than be a checkout clerk. There is a stopping point however and this is where the problem begins with selling off commissions and a scorecard. Sales reps become less interested and just want to get them out of store as soon as possible providing horrible customer service not to mention creating a negative experience for their customers.

One day I was peer coaching another sales rep at the demands of my managers to sell more products relating to the scorecard since this rep was in the red. Usual story customer walks in says I want to buy this device and if its not something a rep gets paid "more" on or not on the scorecard they go into the usual motions of discovery. In this instance the customer cut the sale rep off stating "I don't want you to sell me anything I just want this phone and nothing else." At this point the customer obviously does not want to be sold to and just wants to leave with what they originally came in for. Instead of stopping and understanding the customers needs the rep kept pushing or more like forcing the customer into purchasing the device that suited their paycheck and scorecard ranking. Because of this the customer became upset and left the store without the device they had originally came in for. Before I could begin to coach the rep on what they could have done better she turned to another sales rep and said, "well at least my numbers don't get hit now". My blood began to boil at the sound of the words hitting my ears and I wanted to lash out at the rep for making that statement. Before I could I remembered how I had to coach the rep, likewise, coming across, as drill sergeant would not be very effective. To be honest I didn't feel very comfortable addressing the rep so I decided to bring it up with management to see what they thought.

I didn't exactly get the results I was hoping on from my manager when I brought it to her attention she was drinking the company Kool-aid when I brought it to her attention or she wanted to make her stores numbers looks better. I snapped back stating this was not the right thing to do for the customers, that we were putting business interests ahead of customer interest (equivalent to the Obama administration placing social issues i.e. environmental a.ka. Solyndra ahead of business interest, which has proven not to work out in the long run). My manager began to explain how our company only cares at any one particular time about particular products that make the company money. My blood had just hit boiling point with that statement, management just straight told me to my face they would rather a customer not purchase the device in this store but online or in another store so that our numbers would look better on the scorecard. Its fraud, its unethical, it lacks integrity which happened to be one of our companies core values. Management was supposed to be where I could turn for help if I saw a problem that needed fixing and they failed to correct the issue. As I began to walk out ashamed of the answer I just received my manager told me she would sit down with the sales rep and get her side of the story and if need be take corrective action on anything she may have done wrong. I would have felt better if management didn't make a habit of always sitting down with trouble some employees and never doing anything about it because they help the bottom line.

Sales are not the only thing that is affected by working off commission, when service or troubleshooting comes through the door reps never want to do it. Management always coaches us to embrace tech and service transactions by trying to turn them into sales. It is a great idea honestly seeing how the majority of the time all we do is service transactions. A big portion of my sales actually come off of service transactions seeing how the market is completely saturated with cell phones customers aren't exactly walking adding lines day in and day out.

In the area I work there is an Apple retail store right around the corner from where I work and sales reps love the fact they can use the excuse sorry *"we cant fix that you have to go to Apple"*. Those reps also make excuses when management asks them why they have not sold any tablets this month to say *"because they always go to the Apple store to buy them"* and have no idea why they go to the Apple store. With service comes sales, don't believe you should go to a Firestone Auto Care store, customers go in for a simple oil change routinely which is fast quick and easy but will eventually drive off with a new set of tires costing them around $1,000 dollars. Sales reps where I work seem to neither have the patience nor care causing discrete exchange and horrible customer service.

Case in point, man comes in because his sim card allowing him to get LTE data speeds on his iPad isn't working. The rep realizes he has it on a prepaid account paying $30 dollars a month for 2GB of data and begins to pitch how he can save $20 dollars a month by activating it on a post pay account (fancy term for billing it to his phone bill). She begins to pitch the benefits and does a pretty good job except the customer declines and just wants his iPad to start working again. After hearing those words the rep loses all interest and decides to send him to Apple. Upon the customer leaving she says to the greeter " *he didn't want to add a line so I said you can go to Apple"*. Being as opinionated as I am I wanted to drill her for doing what she did, but decided to bite my tongue and keep thinking she was an idiot.

He came back later in the day with the new sim card because Apple couldn't activate it at their store. I was the fortunate one to have to activate it this time around while the other sales rep stood by just watching. What she didn't notice however was the new screen, protector, and case that he had on the iPad. What I thought was going to be a simple an easy activation ended up being another hour of technical support due to a glitch in the system. He was aggravated, upset, and above all else insanely annoying. I just kept my composure and decided to kill time by demoing my Jambox Bluetooth speaker to him. When I finally figured out a work around to activating his iPad he decided to purchase not just the Jambox but also the BIG JAMBOX! It is a $324 dollar speaker after taxes that sound like a private concert in your home living room. So instead of taking an hour out of an eight-hour day this sales rep lost out on a new case, screen protector, and a BIG JAMBOX. The total revenue she lost out on was over $500 dollars, which is ironic since one we get paid on it, and more importantly get weighted on the scorecard (the goal is $80 per hand set, she missed out on over $500). Like I said before, with service comes sales, it may be a grueling process to get there but people respect the fact when you go out of your way to help them, what goes around comes around

Chapter 3:Cynical People

At home one night watching House with a case of Blue Moon beer after a long stressful day full of service complaints from customers either because their devices were not working, billing errors, or McDonalds messed up their order and they feel the need to yell at me (actually happened once to be honest). It's not uncommon at the end of the night for retail employees where I work to want to go drink to take the edge off. Actually it would be pretty uncommon for us not to do it, likewise I don't hangout with my coworkers anymore. Working in retail has made me realize people in society are cynical and retail doesn't bring out the worst in people but their true self.

After my third beer I received a phone call from a good college friend J.C. Crum. When he asked how I was doing I explained to him how life was good but I had given up on people to do the right thing. Each and everyday I have to deal with customers walking into the store with a problem and begin to either yell or speak to me like I am one of their serfs. Its completely unnecessary for anybody to treat workers in the service industry the way people do. Sometimes I wonder if it would be smart to start hiring psychiatrist, after all we have to listen to people's problems more often than anything else. After a long awkward pause his response was simple *"mike you cant just go and give up on people no matter what you see everyday"* maybe he is right maybe I am, but employees still shouldn't have to put up with the way people treat us.

Its not so much one person comes in and yells at me and I cant handle it and try to make them happy before they leave (no matter what you do upset customers probably aren't going to be happy anyways). It is consistently one after another trying to kill them with kindness, smiling and apologizing to them because their device isn't working due to **user** (*there is a reason "user" is in bold*) error. A customer can say the rudest comments towards me and if I snap back at all they will ask for a manager and explain a very bias story about what happened (i.e. fail to explain why I said what I said to them). No matter what that person said to me I am dead wrong and there is nothing I can do about it. I ask my managers if we can start setting expectations with rude customers from the start that there not going to speak to us like this if they want any help at all. My managers and corporate trainers alike state how we cant, we have to ensure every person a great experience or tell us not to take it personally. Personally I think they are morons, I don't take it personally one bit, its just after eight hours of being yelled at it just gets old after awhile. Furthermore, I realize even though nobody says it at work the customer is always right, however I have taken it upon myself to start setting expectations with customers.

I'm not going to keep writing this chapter telling you customers yell, demean, or even bully us at times even though it isn't right. We ultimately are at blame for the reasons why customers do become upset at times with are policies, but that is because we created an environment in the beginning where we do everything for them. The first smartphones created were Blackberry mobile devices, or if you have to fix them constantly than you know them as Crapberry devices. However, they do serve there purpose for email functions for corporate and consumer use. It is super easy to set up email on those devices since all you have to do is enter the email address and passwords and it automatically gets set up through Blackberry email servers. Now like anything else, adapting and evolving will always be at the forefront of evolution (Blackberry was not however, just ask their shareholders). New developers began making smartphones that allowed you to do the same functions such as Google Android operating system and the Apple iPhone IOS operating system.

As cool as theses devices are its not exactly easy to add email on to these devices if the customers email servers aren't wireless (Gmail, Hotmail, Yahoo, MSN) so if you are reading this book and currently use a different email domain than the four listed above **SWITCH** or do it yourself (I speak on behalf of all cellphone sales reps). For instance, corporate or small business email domains have their own specific server addresses as well as different port numbers for the two different operating systems (ios and android). Where the problem comes in is when the customer switches to one of these devices and request us to put their corporate, small business, or some really weird email domain on their new device. Likewise, very timidly knowing the majority of customer reactions will be negative inform them *"we cant put that email on your phone"* then inform them to contact their IT department at work. I never knew how annoying it was to be told that until I myself went to see the doctor about my knee pain and accidently set it up with an holistic doctor; I was told to Google my symptoms and sent on my way (imagine if my left arm was numb).

People just don't shrug their shoulders and accept the answers to the solutions you give. Same principal when having to explain to your boss why your performance isn't where it should be, they don't care they just want to see results. So when you say no to a customer it is usually followed by comments such as *"I don't understand the last person was able to do this"* or *"I can't go anywhere until my email is put on this device"* if you ask me its rather annoying day after day. From hear you explain to them why we can't do it but used to be able too but people could honestly care less really they just want their device to work. It's funny how when people are lazy and try to do things quote un quote the easy way they cause themselves to do more work. For instance, rather than go to the IT department and take two minutes to set up their email customers would rather spend two hours in the retail store while we search Google looking for the correct settings (don't believe, become one of these customers). While this goes on we get to hear the customer complain incessantly and whether or not we get their email working will usually leave frustrated and frazzled rather than say thank you for wasting two hours of both of our time (being polite, they are actually wasting two hours of my time). Finally, having worked in this position for some time now I have come to expect certain expectations in certain instances, I only wish we could set realistic expectations for customers rather than have a customer is always right mentality.

Email isn't the only subject matter that reveals people true selves. We have two different replacement options for customers who come in with their devices not working. Neither one ever really satisfies the customer but they can be pretty helpful. If the device is under warranty and has a problem we cant fix we can send them out a CLNR (certified like new replacement). If it isn't covered under the manufacturers warranty than if they have insurance they can file a claim and get it overnighted to them (for their upmost convience I might add i.e. not very cost effective for the company).

Around twenty times a week (rounding down of course) a customer comes in with either a cracked, lost/stolen, or watered damaged device that obviously doesn't work. I really do wonder what goes through customers mind when they are driving to the store. Part of me thinks they think of ways to work around the system, another part of me thinks there legitimately going to get another device (for free I might add). I will give you three different examples of customers upset about replacement options on their devices.

1.) Cracked Screen

Me. How can I assist you today?

Customer: I dropped my phone and cracked my screen.

Me:Ahh sorry about that I hate when then happens, follow me back here so we can look at your options.

Customer: Ok, I have been a customer for over 15 years

Me (thinking): One we have only been a company for 12 years and two oh boy here we go.

Me: So it appears you declined insurance and because you cracked the screen its not covered under the manufacturers warranty so your options are 1.) Pay full retail value for a new device, 2.) Purchase a certified pre-owned device, 3.) Or add a line to your account to get a device at the discounted retail price.

Customer: YOU MEAN TO TELL ME YOUR NOT GONNA GIVE ME A FREE PHONE, I HAVE BEEN A CUSTOMER FOR OVER 15 YEARS (again only been a company for 12) I WANT A MANAGER!!!!

ME: OK......

* After about 20 minutes of yelling and expressing frustration about breaking her phone she leaves exactly with the options I gave her.

2.) <u>Lost/Stolen</u>

Me: How can I assist you today

Customer: My phone was stolen

Me: Ahh sorry to hear about that come with me so we can look at your options. Great it looks like you have insurance so let me get you the information so you can file a claim.

Customer: Wait, you mean I cant just come in here and get a new phone?

Me: No we give you the insurance information than you call them and pay the deductible…..

Customer (interrupting me): wait wait wait wait I have to pay a deductible…..why have I been paying for insurance the past six months….

Me: You pay the monthly fee than the deductible so you don't have to purchase it for full retail value which is $650 dollars.

Customer: This is a crock of s***

Me: Please keep your voice down please sir

Customer: HOW BOUT YOU NOT TELL ME WHAT TO DO ALRIGHT, THIS IS BULLS*** YOU KNOW THAT....SO THERE IS NOTHING ELSE YOU CAN DO FOR ME.

Me. These are your options sir.

Customer: YOU KNOW WHAT JUST CANCEL MY INSURANCE

Me: If I cancel the insurance than you cant get another device without paying $650 dollars.

Customer: Don't care I'm leaving this company

Me: Ok well we don't want you to go but if you leave us for another carrier you will have to pay a $250 early termination fee.

Customer: hahaha any other ways you guys are gonna screw me over.

Me: Nope!

*customer took the insurance card, been coming into the store complaining ever since.

3.) <u>Water Damage</u>

Me: How can I assist you today?

Customer: My phone isn't working

Me: Ok well lets take a look (one of the first things I ever do is check for the water indicators)

Me: You have water damage on your phone, pretty bad actually, see that red dot that looks like Mars right here, it should be bright white.

Customer: Water damage how did I get that?

Me in my mind: Hmmmmm you got it wet?????

Me: Could be a lot of things such as moisture, dropping in water, steam, baby putting it in its mouth.

Customer: None of that has happened, it hasn't been anywhere near water…

Me:I fully trust you didn't do anything wrong but the water indicators have gone off which voids the manufacturers warranty, good news is you have insurance to file a claim the deductible will be $170 dollars.

Customer: Why do I have to pay a deductible if I have been paying the monthly fee….

Me in my mind: What insurance doesn't have a deductible….see how this gets old after awhile

Me: You pay the monthly fee so you don't have to pay full retail in the event you have to file an insurance claim.

Customer: THIS IS COMPLETELY RIDICULOUS YOU KNOW THAT YOU
NEED TO FIX MY DEVICE.

Me in my mind: Sure Ill just take a blow dryer to that

Me: Sorry we cant fix this we need you to file a claim so
that you can get another device.

Customer: BUT I DIDN'T GET THE PHONE WET….

Me: I understand that but somewhere somehow the device did
get wet I'm sorry.

Customer:NO IT DIDN'T!!!!!

Me: I'm not trying to accuse you of anything I simply
stating the fact of the matter is the water indicator has
gone off.

Customer: I cant believe this I hate this company.

Me: I'm sorry would you like me to get you the insurance
information.

Customer: Yes…

* twenty minutes of getting yelled at and the customer
ended up doing what I informed them what she had to do
right from the start, talk about efficiency in the
workplace.

Furthermore, instead of training employees to handle angry customers or conditioning society to accept the fact this is just the way the retail industry is we need to start setting more expectations for customers. There is no excuse for treating workers in the service industry the way people do. As progressive as society is moving it is about time for change in the way business is conducted in the service industry. Not accepting the way customers treat service employees may cause them to move to a different company, but those people will eventually treat the next employee like the same as the last, if we all make a stand now just like anything else they have to succumb to the change. The point of this chapter is not to say retail employees provide horrible customer service to customers (which does happen a lot) but rather to explain how customers who complain about receiving horrible customer service had that experience for a reason. Retail employees work very hard everyday, and have to listen to a lot of people's problems considering they have their own to deal with. Furthermore, next time you hear of a friends bad experience in a retail store ask yourself why your friend had that experience, if you don't care and think we should have done more regardless, well sorry to make you read this chapter.

Chapter 4: Bigger pockets to sell out of

In any sales job your managers are going to coach you on how not to sell out of your own pocket. Seeing how retail employees make a lot less money than the customers they serve, and customers especially the ones with money aren't exactly looking to spend it all at once (ironic, the people with money don't like to spend it, don't tell Barack Obama I would hate for him to raise their taxes) makes it a difficult task. Any suggestions (aka excuses to management) will be quickly countered with statements like *"sell the value"* or my personal favorite *"excuses time is over…figure it out"* great suggestion ill make sure to give seminars with this kind of advice. I never learned how to sell out of my own pocket; instead I purchase the most expensive quality products so I am able to sell more of them.

Most of my co-workers always comment on the fact I buy so many expensive accessories. Likewise, I comment on the fact I am one of the highest grossing sales rep in the western United States with a big paycheck. However, the products I am most passionate about at work are the accessories! What is a device without toys to use with it?

Makes a big purchase much easier to justify for someone, after all you don't buy an xbox without any games to play.

What is frustrating the most is when sales rep brings out a big huge bin of accessories (more frustrating when they don't put them away) filled with the cheapest generic accessories. It is usually followed with them coming into the back room shouting some obscenity about how the customer didn't purchase any accessories (I can only imagine why). One thing great sales rep do is adopt best practices from other reps and management makes sure to encourage reps to take on this philosophy (believe me you have no idea what the meaning of beating a dead horse means until you have heard this a trillion times). However, few reps do, actually a few minority actually do causing everyone who performs and management of course to ask why reps don't pick up on best practices.

There idiots, it's the only explanation to be completely honest with you. Watching someone repeat a practice with continual success while you continually fail should prompt a person to change his or her habits. For instance, if continually running the ball up the middle against the University of Oklahoma isn't working Oklahoma State will start throwing the football to get into the endzone. The only explanation to why sales reps do not alter their habits is because they are idiots or they are lazy. Countless times I have peer coached my coworkers about selling more expensive accessories to customers. It is not being greedy or shady; there is a reason why some products are more expensive than others. Regardless of what some entitled idiot trainer (who may or may not have been a high performer when he was a sales rep says) you do get what you pay for.

One of the perks of selling the accessories I sell to customers is that I only pitch four of five. Its not because I am bias but because I have tested that many cases, screen protectors, cases, Bluetooth devices, wireless speakers, portable chargers, car chargers (which are like cheese burgers for a human for a phone keep in mind). I know which products will work well for a customer and which ones will not be beneficial for a customer because they suck. Most people think I am egotistical or entitled since I value my opinion over theirs when it comes to selling (anything really) accessories (I am egotistical and good at whatever I decide to do so get over yourself). It doesn't however explain why people don't listen to me when I give them advice.

The retail director of the area I work in calls me the Jambox King! The Jambox is a wireless Bluetooth speaker that can play movies, music, and phone calls through it. It is superior to any other device when it comes to sound quality. I generally sell around twenty Jawbone Jambox every month. In case you are saying so what big deal there are two different speakers, the Jambox and the BIG JAMBOX! The Jambox is priced at $199.99 while the BIG JAMBOX IS PRICED AT $299.99 (so its pretty impressive that I sell the quantity that I do). I often help other reps not only sell the Jambox but other expensive accessories, except I never hesitate to ask reps why they don't continue to pitch expensive accessories every time. Most of the time they shrug their shoulders and say *"I don't know"* (once again another reason they are idiots or lazy, just ask the French why they don't convert to capitalism). Below I will give a detailed example of a rep having all the right reasons to sell higher price accessories but simply not doing it.

Rep: So here are all the different options for cases and screen protectors (literally close to twenty different cases in that bin).

Customer: UHHHHHHHH I think I am going to hold off on a case for now thank you (obviously overwhelmed at the fact of having to choose between twenty cases).

Rep: Ok (type of sales rep that should have never been hired)

Me in my mind: What an idiot to just stop pitching accessories after the first objection.

Me: (Swooping in like Superman, literally I kinda think sometimes I am) Are you sure you don't want to get a case and screen protector that phone is made of glass on both sides if you drop it, it will shatter immediately.

Customer: (thinking) uhhhhhhhhhh

Me: I recommend the Mophie Juicepack case since it is the most durable protective case we offer but at the same time keeps your phone charged for an additional twenty hours. If you don't want this case we have the Otter Box commuter series, which is slim, but durable, there a You Tube video of throwing this out of a window twenty stories up, the case is destroyed the phone survives. Finally we have this (any generic case but the point was limiting the options), which is a super durable case but allows you to pull the back off so that you can dock it without having to take the phone out of the case. These are also screen protectors I recommend (Zagg screen protectors) these are scratchproof tear proof and peel proof. For any reason they scratch, tear, or peel you will get another one for free no questions asked (notice I didn't say the prices of any of these cases).

Customer: Hmmmm what is the price of this Mophie Juicepack case?

Me: Its $79.99 but if you get a screen protector and case we can give you 20% off of all your accessories.

Customer: What would the price come down too?

Me: If you purchased the case, screen protector, and car charger you would get the Mophie Juciepack case for $59.99 (accessories over $80 dollars only get discounted twenty dollars) Zagg screen protectors for $14.99 usually $29.99 (price tag that always comes on them for some reason but always rings out for $19.99 before discount), and your car charger will come down to $22.49 from $29.99 for a total accessory sale of $97.17 (the goal is $80 per device sale).

Customer: Ok ya I think Ill take those accessories.

Rep: Sure let me go get them (hmmmm why didn't they bring them out to begin with)

Me: Do you listen to a lot of music?

Customer: Ya I do actually

Me: Have you heard of this wireless Bluetooth speaker called the Jambox?

Customer: No (not that I give them the option to say yes or no)

Me demoing the Jambox: (first Katy Perry Teenage Dream for the bass of course and Battle Los Angelos for the action scenes)

Customer: Wow

Me: OH YA YOU CAN EVEN HAVE A PHONE CONVERSATION USING THIS DEVICE!!

Customer: I want one of those!

Me: Red or Black?

Customer: Black (most often, they usually return the red within the fourteen day return policy).

Me: Ok let me go get that for you, just to let you know now that you are getting the Jambox if you get one more accessory you will get all of your accessories 30% off instead of twenty.

Customer: What other accessory do I need?

Me inside my mind: If only we had additional accessories.

Me: (in this instance fyi) You should purchase this Jawbone Era Bluetooth headset, it is designed to only let the person you are talking to hear what you are saying hence the term "jaw" in Jawbone.

Customer: How much is that?

Me: It normally is $129.99 but you will get it for $97.98, I highly recommend this product when you are driving. I was in a motorcycle wreck 3 months ago because someone on a cellphone hit me when I was driving (I honestly was in a motorcycle wreck but not because a person was on a cellphone but because they were an idiot and were gonna miss their exit and decided not to hence running me over…. Furthermore flying in midair regardless of the hype is overrated once you hit the ground).

Customer: Ok ya sure I will get that as well (now we were first at a total of $97.17 after pitching the other devices we were now at a total of $375.14 in accessory sales when the device only cost $199.99)

Sales Rep: Thank you Michael…

Me: Why don't you pitch these devices all the time?

Sales Rep: (after shrugging) I don't know

Me: You should when comfortable start pitching the higher priced accessories more often it will benefit you and your customers.

***rep still doesn't change her habits**

Customers don't purchase these accessories every single time a sales rep pitches them. However, the difference between me pitching these accessories and a rep not pitching them is astronomically different. I will end the month around $80 dollars in revenue per handset and the rep that doesn't will end around $59 or lower. The difference between my style and theirs is that I start high and go low and they start low and finish with nothing. I remember, in the short time working for Firestone one summer the district manager telling me we start high and end low when selling tires in the hope that customer purchase the middle priced tires. Likewise, if these reps even used my philosophy they may not sell the highest priced accessories but would be more likely to sell higher priced accessories as a result. Furthermore, it isn't their fault but management, instead of saying "*ward sells*

these accessories because he says this" they could coach
sales reps to start high and end low significantly
increasing their sales dollars and scorecard rankings
(managers in general could also start hiring actual sales
reps too but I wouldn't want them to work to hard).

Chapter 5: Against the Grain

Not going to lie, I do not expect managers, business executives, professors, or even customers to agree with what I have written in this very short but to the point book. It was told from the point of view from all you know a disgruntled overworked, under paid retail employee. I am not disgruntled; I actually like my job and the people I work with. I am overworked at times but its not a bad thing, hard work builds character, and finally I am not under paid but compensated very well actually and live comfortably allowing me to do the things I enjoy. However, I am not a "*yes man*" meaning I do not succumb to groupthink or think it is healthy.

Just like the scoring on the standardized ACT test high school students take to get into college the majority of the test takers are average. Average isn't a bad thing seeing how most people are average, just look at the test scores. Same principal goes with workers in a company, corporate headquarters are filled with average employees who go along to get along. We live in a who you know not what you know society where being a better politician rather than a smarter person gets you promoted faster.

These are the people I call "*yes men*" (or women) who do whatever the organization says because the organization says to. If I where a recruiter for the United States Army I would know exactly where to go to find potential privates to enlist in the military. We wonder why are businesses are bankrupt and are economy is in a recession. It probably has a direct correlation to promoting people who are not as good at their jobs as the person who rocks the boat. Since the boat rocker makes waves the politician is liked more hence promoted faster.

Imagine how frustrating it is to work for someone who had lower sells numbers, and did not perform as well as you did or smarter than you. It gets even worse when that person becomes your front line supervisor coaching you on why you failed to sell enough of a certain product to meet the company's expectations. The thought running through your mind is I am a better salesperson than you, I sold more of this product and had overall better numbers when we were selling right next to one another. How is this person supposed to coach me because our superiors respected the fact he liked the taste of the Kool-aid when I didn't.

Arguing or having a bad attitude about every new product or policy a corporation rolls out is annoying and counter productive. However, understanding why the company chose to roll out this product or policy but disagreeing with certain aspects and voicing your concern is not but is often taken as such. I am known as an employee who makes waves and rocks the boat, the fact I haven't been promoted shows it as well. What is frustrating is I am a performer and a pretty high performer as well. I do everything the company asks me and do and do it quite well compared to most of the sales reps that work with the company. When the company wanted to push express services (oxymoron) to push tech traffic out of the store I fully understood why the company was pushing the service but disagreed on the execution. It wasn't ready yet and was not any faster but actually took a lot longer. Customers always forgot their passwords, never wanted to do it themselves, and could never figure out what to do. Wait times increased, and sales were lost, but because the company said so we had to do it.

The political employees of course spoke highly of the idea, the majority of employees who don't care but cant find another job complained because they do about everything, and the boat rocker voiced his opinions and concerns about the services. What is ironic is that the Kool-aid drinkers were thanked and praised for being supportive of the service, but people like me were coached about the benefits and why the company is using the service when MY PERCENTAGE WAS HIGHER THAN ANYONE ELSES!!!!!!!!!! Simply because I gave feedback, voiced my discomfort with the service I was looked down upon for it. Rather than succumb to groupthink and do everything the company tells me with a smile on my face I will always voice my opinion for the good of the company whether management agrees with my ways or not.

Furthermore, I am not trying to take away anything from employees who don't rock the boat. Some people don't like to voice their opinions and work 8-5 and there is nothing wrong with it. However, management should know the difference between a performer who has issues with certain products and services and well a terrible employee who complains about everything. Likewise, I encourage and challenge all of you who are reading to not challenge authority but question decision making at times when decisions do not make sense and to remember average people don't rock the boat because they want to jump aboard it.